CUT OF NOON

FREDERICK NICKLAUS

Cut of Noon

David Lewis   New York

ACKNOWLEDGMENTS

When the Circus is Sold, Learning About Leaves, Contract,
The Punished Land, Tropic, These Waking Hands, All
Tenuous Things, Carapace, Cut of Noon, and Afterword
first appeared in *The New York Times.*
Contract appeared also in *The New York Times Book of Verse*
(1970).
From Lips of Shells first appeared in *The New York Herald
Tribune.*
The Slow Travelers first appeared in *Voices.*
Rilke's Panther first appeared in *American Weave.*
Burning of Pears first appeared in *Antaeus.*
Fontana Vecchia, The Road to Castel Mola, The Strait of
Messina, and The Pumice Edge first appeared in *New
Directions 20* (1968).
Balloon first appeared in *The Chicago Tribune Sunday
Magazine.*
Saint John's: Newfoundland first appeared in *The Lyric.*
Levante, Your Secrets Are Those of the Pine Cone, and Tidal
Pools first appeared in *The Mediterranean Review.*

ALSO BY FREDERICK NICKLAUS:
The Man Who Bit the Sun (Poems, 1964)

For Rachel

Contents

CUT OF NOON

When the Circus is Sold

When the circus is sold
and all the animals
are old fire-breathers padding down
the corridors, through stripes of sun-
light cancelling out their own

stripes under high, barred windows.
When the circus is sold
and the old
animals are waiting in rusted cages
by rail spurs, waiting for the boys

to protect them with crating
from the rain.
When the circus is sold
and bars drip rust onto the tracks'
rust, and the doors hang open—

watch the animals walk out,
see their proud walk.
Each eye holds its separate drop of sun
drawn from the daylight, licked into a tongue
to lash you back

into your cage,
toward the corners of your eyes.
Crate me against the winter rain,
and whistle up
along the soundless orange tracks

a pounding train.
And we are told we will be let out,
to carry our bones
through corridors, through stripes of sun.
The circus is long since sold.

The Profligate Remember

Last light, containless in tinted globes
suspended in string nets, slow,
revolving prisons for the palpable,
mottles bricks and beams of the patio.
Against the sky
the globes darken with the long-dry ground
that audibly absorbs the old rain
I pour from their thin throats.

They hold me in a world of other sound,
clasped by an afternoon
when the monkey clambered to a planting basket
to caw complaint beneath the dripping beams.
While the stale catch of rain
warmed and cooled, warmed again
with the days and nights, the white clothesline
hung desolate, unclimbed, as now
while the ground drinks old rain like festal wine.

So the light, the light must gradually go,
and memory flash through the mind
spear, lizard-tongue sharp from seeming confine
to blur the actual world here:
the house, this table, myself in a chair,
merge in three turning globes of glass,
one with last light
whose gold thought hoarded in burnished mintage
of the sea grape tree, with profligate gesture,
leaf by coin leaf spends itself toward night.

Making the Rounds

Peering down stairwells, opening closet doors,
right hand at holster level,
making the rounds,
he is part of each day, accepted
like the filing case, this typewriter, the floor's
familiar loose tile.
Do not see him, accept him as the sole
meets the pavement, and the file
receives the letter in its endless toll.
The shadow in the stairwell, the closet's noose
do not exist. He is just
making the rounds,
facing the well.
His plumb stare
sounds all the emptiness in hell.

From Lips of Shells

From lips of shells past mariners heard
their many ports, clapped hearthstone hands
in hospital wards, flushed memory's

raucous birds—made trees explode
inside their brains and black the blurred
days marked downward in their dun blood;

a torpor the youngest half understands,
while the oldest seems to sleep. The sea's
first kneeling child, shell carved to ear,

its lost sound cadent to last breath,
found dead here; foetal, age-ringed knees
updrawn, and yellow as boles of trees

fresh cut for shipyards, naked rings
outward counted to the final year.
All dusk's flushed birds roost round his death.

Incubus

The road wakes me: sound
of a horse walking hollowly.
Mist on the fields
coils out of itself.
My tongue has not moved.
It ties no knots
for itself to unravel.
It lies simply,
as you lie.
Sun shafts despoil mist
across the fields.

The horse is terrified.
It veers from the lane,
bolts through wet grass
to the bogs beyond.
It is struggling to its death
in the steaming peat.
The noise of its agony
half wakes you.
I watch the unquiet shadow of a fern
on the wall. And our moving tongues
make no words.

Rainwalk in the Forest

The house and its field on top of the hill
are in a cloud; and the forest falling away
in all directions to the lower lands
seems but the margins of an unmoving cloud.
We take a rainwalk in the forest,
sound close in needles and snapping twigs,
each raindrop poised and ready at leaf edge,
attenuate toward the leaf below,
distinct from the hushed, the timeless rain
heard ceaselessly, yet not at all.
Direction is lost in the forest—
but we have made a circle
back to the house, to its field on the hill.
East? West? North? South?
The house has turned full axis in our absence.
Mysterious things can happen in a cloud.

Learning About Leaves

Learning about leaves
in winter, in the first class, snow heavy on the sash
and the light voice of chalk in the room
speaking the careful order of things:
palmate, runcinate, lyrate in a row.
And the scar on the hand's back
healed, as the great swirling leaf-horn of the forest
spun down, tilted to the forest floor,
crinkled past autumn, drank back into the earth
now covered with white crust.
The hand is moving, moves toward warm
waking.
Palmate, runcinate, lyrate
move singly on the sky.
The scar reopens.

Cayo Hueso

Island of pirates and wreckers, named for bones
found strewn on cutting coral; of sun,
of trees leaning landward, a swirl of cloud,
brown rocks where waves fold over themselves
and trickle rake-straight rivulets down.

Deface its buildings, stripe its beaches
with black oil traces; make deepest cisterns
reek their secrets to the glaring sun.
Stepping sleepward down, emerge
to the worst levels of the town.

In geology of the brain,
all cloying semblance now stripped away,
charred sea fronts sift into a torpid bay;
the sand grain grafted on the vengeful sun
is a vision of railyards, of locomotives

coupling by night, of gondola cars where fronds
traced in coal remind of time's layers,
time's concealments, and the fragility
that moves four eyes when one leaf falls
through sunshafts locked like rake teeth on the sea.

The Water Tower

No one can tell you when he came
to take up habitation here,
in the water tower above the town.
But all agree he's never come down.
It seems as if his shearing off
of the tower, then his hit or miss
hurling of boulders might as well
be lost beyond all geologic time.

I saw the tower first at dusk
against the sky, against the sea's
broad palms that burned when boulders sank
sizzling from his volcanic thrust.
Now the rat-run edge of the tank
that holds the boulders of his labor
sounds only to the slowest breeze
on vines and weeds. A rusted-out

bent metal stack is propped to catch
the last of red drained from the sky,
though years ago someone had said
that fires kept in his stove breathe on.
I know he's long since stumbled down
his own declivities and died.
Tonight, wedged deep between the boulders,
his pithless bones must catch the wind,

slow, rumored, falling out of time,
beyond the people of this town.
Here none remember the carrion
birds circling low to tell them how
he fell. Tomorrow I will climb
and wave to all: "Come see, come see!"
my hands with any weed or vine
from dark stone pockets waving free.

There I will put the bones together,
my herald not the carrion
birds, but the first light, and a trace
of smoke above his stove, the last
wind raking past the safe, dead ashes.
And dangerous seeds will share my sill
to germinate in their own time.
The day will be so warm, so still.

Blood Rain

This is blood rain
pounding them low,
to the ground itself.
Dust of the air
beads the cowled,
hunched figures.
Its blight stains
their bread.
Then sun dries
blood rain,
baking thin cauls
of clay over eyes
open and dead;
each hand
raising to lips
the crust stained red,
in a land
dust only.
And blood rain.

Under Cancer

In a darkening room, in the slow time after
the fall of need, we listened to the cat claw out his lungs.
His cough sounded down
to us, listening side by side, as from well or crypt,
dripped on by the stones, chained to the fierce
progress of his poisoned cells.

His breath caught dryly as the scrape of palms
along the rain gutters clogged with fronds, the long needles
raining from pines that rocked behind the house.
The parrot cracked its seeds; gulf wind swept the tiles.
And the cells made clear progress,
coursing their poisons round the cat in his lungs.

Stylized as lids of sarcophagi
we lay, side by side, hands
pressed not in prayer, nor reaching any sky
ever. For we lay separate, each alone
and tracing for self the edges of his cough,
the cat in his lungs clawing for air.

And the cells made swift progress,
headlong rushing with wind from the gulf, its sudden
recoil, the small snap of a seed,
then the rushing on, through pines bent above the house,
needles of the black Australian pines
sewing the cat back up in his lungs.

Leopardi

The thing I noticed first was not the room
itself, its view of sea and cliffs contained
within deep arches, nor its shadowed cool
of tiles and plaster walls, but *Leopardi*
spelled on the blackest book spine, leaning toward me.

So he has stalked me even to this town
above the pleasure coast that runs away
from Naples killing with its cholera,
the coast where even to pronounce it—death—
becomes an obscene rasping of the breath.

Ignoring him, and Naples, and the dead
volcano's peak, not hearing after dark
the rats that run along the trellis tops,
half-blinded by the day's prismatic light,
I will forget him and his horrible night.

He waits me though, in sound of surf that crumbles
shoreward, and softly as volcanic ash
half parts my sleeper's lips, and calls in wind
that wakes me to the darkness and myself.
Then I take Leopardi from the shelf

and read him on the balcony, the lamp-
thrown shadows twisted as his back, until
far at the farthest angle of my view
Naples emerges, gray and filmy shape,
the dread miasma I shall not escape.

Once more I pack to leave a paradise,
pay up the bill and tip the porters, start
back down the sunny road that brought me here,
my life once more his night of Recanati,
the dark within me that I cannot flee.

Contract

The hall clock, metal teethed to metal,
whirs its wheels to keep
sixteen chimes before the hour
that tolls itself to sleep.

I heard the clock when summer wind
creaked branches, heard the slow
addition of its muffled chime.
Now overhead the snow

shifts, swirls on shingles; and the sound
of metal shrunk with cold
strikes with a clearer, harder voice
than summer's. Why hands fold

into each other to be one
is a mystery the house
speaks to itself, board on beam,
and beam to board laid close.

And why a heart in cold contract
with itself can break beyond
the blindness spoken by the hands
of lovers is my bond

kept with the metal, learned from clocks
chiming the night away;
while two together locking hands
must whisper: "Stay. Stay, stay."

The Punished Land

You pulled my hand to the slowness of your heart,
and I, who would not feel the failing of my own
for fear, who could not bear
a hand's first simple reach before
disguises inevitably picked it apart
and left their shards of angry fact—
I pulled my hand away.

In a room encrusted with shells,
over the iced wine called by a name
I cannot remember, in a punished land,
I thought of the many hands
touching harvest, and of the many
unseen fingers of the sea whose shells
now gleamed like porcelain from the rock walls.

Your name comes back to me,
and your first, tentative
reach comes back ten-fold.
I pulled my hand away.
Four grappling hands made two hearts die
and strike their separate ways forever
across the many guises of the day
where any lie can sever.

The Dog's Drowning

described too carefully:
broken ice and unknown hours
in numbing water before you heard
her moans, and knew her missing, and saw
the nostrils only, like a floating
stone.
Why described so carefully?
This was no simple sharing of pain,
for you knew
all rightful loss would be your own,
the dog no longer mine.
You shame me to belief in a woman alone,
my life become desertion,
then indifference.
A bottomed stone is mindless of rings
spreading on the surface,
and the timeless tree not meant for sectioning.
You are unaccountable
for written and widening circles of your blame.
In the dog's death you willed my return.
I wonder if, in another, and another,
in some lasting bole of love,
I must meet you at the end.

Lookout

I wake in the cave, uncertain
of day or of night.
The same stooped light
of a stopped moon or a tiring sun
taps at the cave's mouth.
No lip of sky
burns blue, no breath of close stars
reminds me of the height, of the altitude.

Oil dries in the lamps, and one bent wick
shadowed on rock is taller than my door,
my straw bedding wind-strewn on the floor.
I want to look out, to see if your frozen tracks
are filled with new snowfall,
but weakest light blinds at the cave's mouth.

I want to look out.
This is a great altitude.
If I tethered you here
in a cave by oil-fed light,
the sky was a blue sliver
extracted from my flesh in the morning,
one star breathing close at night.

We shared this cave
divided by a firm chalk line you called the sun's
farthest reach, and I the moon's.
If I starved your mouth and gorged your hairs'
roots with honey,
insects imaginary
crazed you. And I set you free.

I want to look out.
I know you will come back.
A starved beast retraces its own frantic tracks.
We will lie here together
in blind light from the cave's mouth.
You will whisper this to me, in our imagined morning
of a tiring moon and a stopped sun:
"There is a lip of sky
our cave must never kiss." And I will ask you:
"Is it a sliver of blue,
or one breathing star?"

I snap the wick. It curls on its bed of cracked
oil in the lamp's base. I want to look out.
I think a new snow has concealed your frozen tracks,
your way back.
I dreamed the flakes on my lips while I slept.
Day, night, day, night.

Find our way back.

The Descent

The descent past coigns and clefts
of a wave-gutted mountain reaches the smooth sands
opening, bridge to the land's
lights at evening, moving trees of day.
Scarves and banners of the first climb
signal the path. Now they lead back,
and explain their failed promises away.

The coasts and the great winds
led the climb. But rocks speak hollowly. And the sea
itself tilts uneasily under the sky: water in a bowl
offered by uncertain hands. Purple roads
and wind-carried scents lead on.
There is no choice at the crossroads; and the man
swinging from the gibbet is eyeless still.

Scarves and banners are stuffed between stones
of a roadside wall, above the plain
where crossroads close on choice. And a chain in the hand
flagellates no promise from the wind.
One by one the sea's reflections are driven from the cells.
Charred sticks and the bones of fish
are shape and shadow across the new land.

The Slow Travelers

Needles fall on unknown flowers,
morning lapses to noon,
heat curls leaves to its palpable self.
The postman, with his air of ancient ritual,
brings letters for the all
but nameless.
                    Afternoon
dips into evening, when the spent green
of day bursts briefly beyond itself.
The white fence glows to the edge of blue.

Wait in the room now,
hear them go by, the slow travelers,
their soft steps on the road
before the house. They seem to pause
at the gate. Dark fronds
lean close to their waiting.

They stand a little while and then go on.
Walk to the low gate;
they have left no trace on the road.
Creak the letter box open
on its black heart;
the increased beating of your own
fills the dark.

Stars last long. Your hard, imploring
fingers half close on emptiness.
The palm goes silent on the eaves,
the road finds dawn, whose gray, immense
hands are suppliant as your own, as leaves.

Rilke's Panther

Though Rilke strays down long Dalmatian coasts,
delaying in lent castles, treading their hushed parquet
in his lean slippers,
he is forever vagrant in every city,
frequenter of clinics,
stroller to the zoos.

Rilke before the panther's cage
sees the panther pad in slow
circles round the pivot of a yet unbroken will,
wind to the pitch of its elegant rage.

Rilke, through bronzed leaves
of European autumn wanders on.
Cities tremble on their iron webs;
wind rattling the perfect page
of his last finished poems is an iron wind.

The panther wanders, wanders in rage.

Four silent years now settle on his mind.
Tubular metal of cage or gun
in his gutted sensibility are one.
The slow circles wind
tighter, tighter to the unsinging core.

—Till it is shattered with his call for answer!
Song rushes over rocks down the long Dalmatian shore,
tethers to stone the panther's rage:
each pliant tendon of the finally freed
out-running panther prisoned on the page.

Burning of Pears

The plaster coolness of unfinished rooms,
red bricks sizzling in rusted barrels,
water from the black shale spring
below the pear tree—and the dog first darting
to the lake that began as a widening stream
through a valley of chain-wrapped stumps uptorn.

Patched and cabled but kept alive,
in a sudden storm the pear tree fell at last.
All summer, with hammer and iron wedge,
I split the locked branches, as men
in winter destroy a work of years,
desperate cordage for the warmless heart.

The house has settled, grown easy with the earth,
its rooms long finished.
The dog maunders down a lawn clean of pears,
nuzzles the pearwood on the terrace.
I have split then corded the years away,
my face in the glass finds the lake's frozen face.

I would smell once more, heavy on the air,
the sogged brown pears that rotted on the lawn,
long fallen, punctured on rake prongs, pulled
far down the slope, to the low fires, the brown
fact of autumn acrid on the air,
dissolved across the valley that is forever gone.

Fontana Vecchia

What can they know of us,
though we remain
in olive and almond trees contending on the slopes,
and in the low
unlighted hills of Calabria close
across the Strait. And with the slow
vigilant arcing of the moon.

What can they know of us,
waiting out the rain,
talking in the red-tiled rooms of our house,
while near along the coast
that little two-master tarries in the cove,
and sunlight wedges through the easy rain.
What can they know of us,

and of our hands' quest half the night
who see us buried in bright
tendrils worming through the cypresses.
What can they know of us: two ghosts
haunting what should have been our own —
Shall we tell them a little,
our pilgrims waiting out the rain?

The Road to Castel Mola

I have rested long enough, sitting halfway
up the mountain, on a curve
under Castel Mola.
I read initials and a recent date
scratched on cactus leaf.
The sea below, lips open then closed
white on that tressed, square rock,
makes broken mouthings to the sky.

I thought I would be in Castel Mola now,
sitting by some round-stoned dusty square
that I shall never know,
nor drink the slow beer
past noon, waiting here, on a low wall, at a sharp
turn of the road under Castel Mola.

Initials and a recent date
scratched on cactus leaf;
someone's spade scraping stone,
a stab of light across the valley,
and this senseless delay before starting down.
I wonder why the big words of the sea
grinding and groining the sweep of the shore
are mimic here,
and a man's curse, his spade dulled on stone,
strikes in air.

Words have rung
to silence on the opposite slopes.
A bird that hung wings wide
and still above the mountain
banks slow-circling from the sun.
The unfeatured sky is white past noon,
the town hidden by the mountainside.

I know I have given up too soon
over a dumb sea mounting a dumb rock
in dubious love; and black
dogs that barked from farms as I climbed
wait by the farms to bark me back.

The Strait of Messina

Awake past dusk to a clanking of bells,
the unreverberate tolling of the town,
I thought of the long corridors,
wooden saints, bronze seductions,
heavy-framed landscapes murky and brown
even in fierce morning light
flawed off the courts where white
unweeded gravel was cut across
by the edging shadow of the eccentric roof.

I listened to the flat-toned bells
commemorate some public death.
The occasional clatter of a train
broke the sea's faint breath; the balcony,
long gorged on too much moonlight, stretched
its iron swan necks to gorge again,
festive on that mourning night
when the sea with a rattle in its throat
relentless, lied to the tractable coast.

Turning away, you watched the squares
of light that edged across the floor,
heard rush of water that took its want
through each rock orifice of the shore;
turning, whispered undulant words
to one lying opposite, dark and close
as mainland hills across the Strait:
turning, whispered to a ghost
words that I had heard before,

whispered duplicate words while bells
cowled round their silenced iron tongues;
and then for half the mourning night
you walked each stair and corridor,
where wooden saints watched bronze seductions
cast forever at their height.
Sleep now between myself and a ghost,
like the sea, long celebrant, that rolls from both
dark lovers, insatiate, still lost.

The Pumice Edge

I push her wheelchair in and out of shops
where travelers meet. She winds the colored scarves
around some saint's white plaster head;
I thumb through postcards, pulling out von Gloeden's
wigged boy called 'Duse,' or the one
called 'Lamp of Love.' The youngest must be dead,
or else an old man nodding in the sun.

After the cities and their many fountains
she brought me here, to live beneath a mountain's
anger masked with snow. The pumice edge
of alcohol or flesh could not erase
her memory, the scarred volcanic land's
reflected face where three drowned children called
to her, held out imploring hands.

She kept their photos in a triptych frame
she carried always, showing them to strangers
in shops or on the street, as well as those
other strangers that we called our friends.
Year after year from different lands they came,
climbing the dusty pathway to our house
hidden by vineyards roped around three hills

of lava earth. For twenty years we drank
with them, and when we were alone
together drank ourselves into oblivion.
One night I woke beside her, and I loathed
myself for taking her. While she slept
again I saw us as a pair of dogs
coupled in lava for some discerning age,

the triptych frame beside us more a relic
like the hearth screen, fire pokers, two chipped glasses,
than the charged receptacle of my rage.
I edged the photos out, stirred flame from embers,
and burned them. While the lonely pre-dawn wind
scattered ashes around us on the floor
I lay beside her, made love to her once more.

A mountain counts its vintages, and kills
halfway sometimes. The stroke that bound her tongue
cruelly kept her memory intact.
But friends forgot. Now I garner from the town
new strangers who will watch her re-enact
with speaking hands and empty triptych frame
the need no drunkenness could ever drown,

new strangers who will listen as I tell
this story, straying like von Gloeden's ghost
along the sea wall where I chance to meet
the boy called 'Duse,' and the one
called 'Lamp of Love,' false-nodding pair
of beggars hooded from the noonday heat,
or waiting past midnight on each steep, stained stair

that links the many levels of the town.
All postcard beggars recognize
me as I pass, hold out imploring hands.
But my heart was moulded to a perfect stone
in those twin furnaces, her hot-tongued eyes.
I have forgotten when my own
were more than chinks into an empty cell.

Ledges

Ledges: cold, silent, empty
Ledges, smooth, unbroken, limestone
Ledges, ivy-shadowed on a summer night.
Glass grinding brick, long cluttered
Ledges, broken, up stairwells, in slanting walls.
Ledges for escaping hands.
           and the secret, dizzy
Ledges in the heart and brain
Heavy with their secret rain.
Ledges zigzag down, down the dark stair —
    stomach — heartwell,
Breaking the wrist's arch; nail-scraped
Ledges for secret leaping.
Ledges.

Sea Lanes

It was a time of the sea's presence
always, in many places made ever the same
with that sad weaving of sea lanes together
in ancient ports. And we imposed our moment,
furtively as figures stalking the sea wall
nightly; by day the moving eyes in palm courts
under enameled, silent clocks.
　　　When the blue burned off the sky
we sought the cool, dark corners of ragged talk,
desultory under the carved beams, the breeze
failing through dry fronds.
Two small, dark presences always near the sea.
　　　She could have passed in light,
choosing the black olives from the market baskets,
gathering iris on the headlands after.
In our wandering I did not glimpse her once,
my shadow compliment to another.
　　　In a hard-lit land, the waves' sound long receded,
the shadow talk become a memory,
I found her, and we broke the land's meshed lock.
The wind woke in the palms.
　　　She sleeps now, under the tapestry
of camels and Arabs, shimmering oasis palms
woven on blue oasis water.
Camels and Arabs move ever on.
The clock ticks to a halt. She wakes soon,
gatherer of iris on the headlands
where we watch the sea lanes weave together.

Balloon

All else must fade, this city and its dome,
the dusk of balconies, wind-circling birds
above the gardens and the gardened roofs;
hushed voices, then the vast insistent moan
through squares and byways of the traffic geared
anew for night.
    Turn toward the shadowed room,
forget the dome washed round by dusk's brown tides.
Know you shall always have the afternoon,
and always, in the sun, a yellow balloon
floats past your face, while voices left below
are calling after. You remember how
it rocked one moment in a crossing breeze,
and then, string trailing, pulled straight for the sun.

All else must fade.
    Turn toward the shadowed room.
And if I toss a coin or drop my keys
into the street, the street not there at all,
my coin or keys might flash forever down
through clear green waters of a bottomless dream.
The moment and the bright balloon were one,
all else was drowned with the consuming sun.

Plums

The plums flicker with low fire,
flames never licking or lashing,
but commingled, almost asleep.
The plums have smooth stones at their centers.

Warring toward the simple need,
we shed the thin mucilage of sheets,
only to draw them up in darkness,
the seed spent.

While we sleep
the wrinkled stone at our center
rains fire upon itself.
Its faint, radial glow
spreads outward through the closed flesh.

In the small-leaved gardens
the plums are beaded with dawn sweat.
From their wooden bowl
they mirror our waking's first awareness,
our wrapped tongues working to raise the sun.

Tropic

Though led by quickened fear
of thunderclouds and lizards,
her walk along the arches
is unperturbed and slow.

Her touch is in the falling
of flowers from their vines,
her voice the muted calling
of birds that know their roosts.

The storm that broke today
on walls of fortresses
flicked cats from sentry posts,
shook torpor off the bay.

Thunder still mutters low,
lizards brooch tile and leaf.
Her face along the arches
moves, unperturbed and slow.

For R. Sleeping

The twin gardens are closed.
Birds sleep in the boughs
heavy above them.
Shadows of the gates
touch across the path's
white crystals.
     Your dream
of beaches and the wind
leaves little porticoes of sand
at corners of the walls.

The twin gardens are closed.
Men with rakes and brooms
might tend them after dawn.
Then tall gates open,
sleeping birds have flown.
Pillars of light support the sun
on crystals of your shattered dream.

These Waking Hands

I followed you, and following, left no trace,
so whitely did my chosen ways unfold
on whiteness that these waking hands erase.

The fire that kept me to your perfect pace
leads searchers, though the last was long since told
I followed you, and following, left no trace.

The searchers who would find us in this place
must wander from their youth till they are old
on whiteness that these waking hands erase.

I am so jealous of your waking face,
the warmth you gave me when, long lost and cold,
I followed you, and following, left no trace.

If they must find us in our bones' embrace,
and carefully from what were blankets rolled
on whiteness that these waking hands erase

pick me from you, the blanket-rot like lace
still clinging, they are searchers far too bold.
I followed you, and following, left no trace
on whiteness that these waking hands erase.

Prophecy

So it is easy. We are young,
finding play in hopeless quest:
my coat and trousers lightly thrown
inside-out across a chair
with haste of love enacted here.
With sleep's quick mercy we are blessed.

Prophetic now, my body groans
unwaking, and the waking taste
is dark: my clothes too neatly hung—
or crumpled crazy-edged as stone,
dropped drunkenly in night alone
with nothing of desire's haste.

Each hour ago alarms have rung
themselves to silence, yet I lie
ferreting out half-thoughts that come
lowering with the weight of stone
across my chest when sleep is gone
to crush the last haste from desire.

I leave you sleeping; light is early
in rooms left incomplete as this.
The haste of love was with us: surely
the habit was an easy one—
ending with me, in you begun,
and small completion from our kiss.

Prophecy II

Waiting in a timeless land
repeated anywhere,
he clenches an ungiving hand
against ungiving air.

Once he ought to sharpen all
his senses on each ledge
and rock. Glintless now, dull
as chalk the metal-edge

thrusting of his intent. Too soon
he found the substitutes:
his tangling blood went cool by noon,
his heart put out no roots

for other nourishment. Made blank,
his brain ignored his death.
Forever feeding on the rank
contagion of his breath,

lovers come in endless lists,
candescent-winged as flies.
See, impotent as clocks their fists,
the claws behind their eyes.

All Tenuous Things

We have grown apart. Your presence is not clear.
We are separate
with habit. I no longer hear
your words. You are accepted like the earth
for sure rough-whorled root, for hill—
rock worth.
You are accepted like the plunging earth.

Seated on this terrace,
all tenuous things grown strong about me,
limb shadow on a painted shutter,
hydrangeas petaled to burst,
I catch you in some random act
recalled, or now:
clearing a picnic table, bending
to gather shells along the shore.
I see you from afar
as at the first,
when custom had not blighted at the core.

Deadlock

It is the way people talk to you:
simply, as light shapes the stone,
evolving one identity.

Or something you must carry around,
arrogant as disease
eating, while light troweled out to light

cements the certain day. Then some one
for the first time must say:
"These are words you will not hear again,

not with your utmost need."
The saw-edge dulls the brain.
It is the way people talk to you,

not your self with its private weight.
That you can self-explain:
first light, flawed noon, the terrible night.

It is the voice edged with fright
for you and not its own
that echoes the enormousness of loss.

Saint John's: Newfoundland

We passed the crooked fishing village,
red, blue, and yellow from the sea,
Latin with children and doorway leaners,
dust and a broken tree.

The first red-gold on the rocky slopes
burned to your climbing Yorkshire joy.
Below, the harbor a mossy pool,
the tethered ship a toy.

We knelt for blueberries. September noon
was bells, noon gun, the blueberries' taste.
You skipped back down by the curving road
I remember, all homeward haste.

The Voice

It waits always, washed with light, a voice
around me holding all distances, but close
as an amulet clasped in my hand.
Though I go far away, the false land
closing behind me, and try many doors,
I am drawn back.

Once the streets were covered with sand
for a king's horses to track;
and once they held deep emptiness
traced on my open palms.

The voice shapes an amulet that calms
my graven sleep, and as I sleep more
it steals away, and leaves its light margins on the shore.

THREE POEMS

I. *Levante*

This is a morning of *levante*,
of the shutter left open, and waking to light
that glares at itself in the bureau mirror;
a morning of balcony doors slamming, of stumbling
    from bed
to pull the shutter against the day
crumbling over Cape Malabata.
Levante scuds on the bay; and the white
town wakes with burro and rooster
below a waning moon.

Malabata. *Mala pata.*
Your simple Spanish joke repeats itself.
Last night we rounded the Cape of Bad Luck.
Now this day looms ahead.
I step back into the room; you stir on the bed
and bury your face against the double glare.
I pull the shutter, and sit beside you.
You do not wake, and I lie back, listening
to *levante* tugging at the doors . . .

listening to a wind I cannot name,
other doors slamming somewhere
above this same sea, on balconies of another white town;
and someone else beside me.
Your body in shadow fills the bureau mirror
where my hands hover, not touching you.
Finding no trace, not leaving one,
they move, reflected and separate, and then, slowly,
come together to cover my face.

* *Mala pata.* Spanish slang for "bad luck."

II. Your Secrets
Are Those
of the Pine Cone

Your secrets are those of the pine cone,
scale on imbricate scale.
Your anger is the tiger's print on a petal;
mine, the storm moving toward a mountain.

We walk apart, my eyes scanning the far coast,
yours drilling the sand underfoot
for the minute breathing place of a clam
revealed as the water moves away.

III. Tidal Pools

You have contended always with a ghost,
watching us now from mists drifting across the mountain,
leaving no track behind us in the sand.
Yet he follows us from water, toward volcanic rock
where we climb among tidal pools—mirrors
that hold us as we lean and watch
clinging snails, mussels, the little fish darting
across our faces.
             Watching too,
he makes no image for you to catch.
I alone see him, repeated in every pool
where I clasp your shoulders or take your hand
one moment against the sky.
And as we walk back, beside the water,
I alone see—our own tracks washed away—
his leading toward us, emphatic in the sand.

—Tangier

Modigliani

I am alone with them all. They surround my solitude
as never before, their blank eyes negating their flesh
that glows with tones of Tuscan earth.
Now I am alone with them all.

This is a cold room, the last of many. January rain
strikes the streets. The wine shops are shuttered.
I am too sick for wine now, but lift my glass.
More vomit and coughing. My daughter stirs in her crib.

Once I walked in circles of fire.
But even then the warmth of flesh, its contours
guiding my brush, my hands, enclosing my sex,
ended in the gray opacity of their eyes.

One brought me scarves and rings,
and I caressed her for brandy among crystals and silks.
Loathing myself, I smashed the mirrors,
and found my way again, sketching strangers in the streets.

I cannot forget the Tuscan earth, and the evening light.
I cannot forget the kindness of one who took me to the
    warm sea,
the shuttered windows, the scraping of palms in the court.
But always the return to wet and cold. Cold rooms and
    random flesh.

This wine is sour on my stomach. I am sick. When will
    you come back?
This is my dream: I stand on a vined pergola, high
    above the city.

Vases of ocher and burnt umber radiate the light
of Tuscan evening. And sound is the sound of
   Italian seas.

When will you come back? You move along the trellises.
Your hand latches the shutters. You lie next to me in
   dim afternoon.
—I wake. You have come back. Your hand is cold and
   wet on my brow.
Warm milk dribbles from my lips. You rock me as I weep.

I am nothing but gray flesh, and a cough that nears
   its end.
Now I am alone with them all. They push you away
   from me,
surround my bed. I cannot breathe, yet they lower
   over me.
And there is no light, none, in the awful opacity of
   their eyes.

Carapace

Straying emptily down
the late day's indifference,
cattle at a cloud's pace
follow the cliff fence

across a sinking sun.
I watch them from my door.
Why have I not moved on?
These battened windows, one

broken oar? From stone
to stone, in fear of self
I go. The tides erase
my tracks each dusk or dawn.

It gleams now from the shelf,
the ugly carapace
I would cast off, as tides
do, yet I pick its sides

clean for the phantom meat
left there, by the tides.
My own dead line my street.
Why have I not moved on?

Cut of Noon

The sun dazes you at your door,
dangling its barbs between the patio beams
like tendrils, twitching your eyes
as you stumble from a dark room
to a day breathing through porous stone
light as pumice and white with heat.
Your fear runs mercury-quick at the rim
of a glass, the cut
of noon confronting you once again
across the flags toward afternoon.
Your fear swells with the lizard's throat,
makes traps of rope from a garden hose,
tastes poison in salt at the rim of the glass,
venom in the tail of an eye.
Your fear is shadow of the self you hang
each day, from a white beam. Your assassin's shadow
moves across the parched grass.

Afterword

The need that led me
straight to the cat's place by the fire
has fed itself away.
Winter thunder makes its low
retreat. Glazed choppings of old snow
free the frozen last imprint
of a cat that curled its claws
as if to strike from self
the fire it could not feel.
Step on step I go,
from drift to melting drift, away from you.
No parting gesture from the curtained window
whose warmth once drew me through the freshening snow.

About the book

THIS BOOK HAS BEEN DESIGNED BY EDWARD AHO
FOR DAVID LEWIS, INC. THE TYPEFACE IS MONOTYPE
BULMER. THE TEXT WAS SET AND PRINTED
BY THE STINEHOUR PRESS, LUNENBURG,
VERMONT. THE PAPER IS CURTIS RAG.
1000 COPIES PRINTED.